AN INSTANT PLAYSCRIPT

WOMEN
OF THE DUST

RUTH CARTER

London
NICK HERN BOOKS

TAMASHA PLAYS

An Instant Playscript

Women of the Dust first published in Great Britain in 1999
as a paperback original by Nick Hern Books Limited,
14 Larden Road, London W3 7ST

Published jointly by Nick Hern Books and Tamasha Theatre Company

Women of the Dust copyright © 1999 Ruth Carter

Typeset by Country Setting, Kingsdown, Kent CT14 8ES
Printed and bound in Great Britain

ISBN 1 85459 448 6

A CIP catalogue record for this book is available from
the British Library

*Funded by an Arts for Everyone grant
from the National Lottery through
the Arts Council of England*

Tamasha Theatre Company

Artistic Directors: Sudha Bhuchar, Kristine Landon-Smith
General Manager: Kathy Bourne

'A major national Asian theatre company producing new writing theatre
that draws from Asian literature and contemporary Asian life in Britain
and abroad.'
London Arts Board

'A highly successful company of national importance, producing high
quality Asian theatre, that is visual, powerful and thought provoking.'
The Arts Council of England

Kristine Landon-Smith and Sudha Bhuchar formed Tamasha in 1989
to adapt *Untouchable* a classic Indian novel by Mulk Raj Anand.
After an extremely successful debut the company has gone from
strength to strength. Tamasha aims to reflect through theatre the Asian
experience – from British Asian life to authentic accounts of life in
the Indian sub-continent, adapting works of literature and classics
to commissioning new work from a range of contemporary writers.

Tamasha Theatre Company, 11 Ronalds Road, London N5 1XJ

Tel. 0171 609 2411   *Fax.* 0171 609 2722
E-mail: general@tamasha.demon.co.uk
Website: http//www.tamasha.demon.co.uk

Women of the Dust was first performed at Bristol Old Vic Studio on 7 October 1992 with the following cast:

PARVATI, MOHINI	Sudha Bhuchar
JAMADAR, HAWKER	Shiv Greval
LALLI	Niki Jhutti
KAMLA, DIMPLE	Shobu Kapoor
DADI, CHARU	Jamila Massey
A.J. THE CONTRACTOR	Rehan Sheikh
MOHAN	Dinesh Shukla
ASHA, NEESHA	Nina Wadia

Other parts played by members of the company

Director Kristine Landon-Smith
Designer Sue Mayes
Lighting Designer Lorraine Laybourne
Composer and Musical Director John O'Hara

Characters

PARVATI, *a female construction labourer, 40 plus*

MOHAN, *Parvati's son, about 20*

ASHA, *Mohan's wife, about 18*

LALLI, *Parvati's husband's brother's daughter – a child bride, 10 plus*

KAMLA, *Parvati's sister in law, about 25*

CONTRACTOR (A.J), *35+*

DIMPLE, *the contractor's wife, 25 plus*

JAMADAR, *site middleman, 24 plus*

DADI, *Parvati's widowed sister in law. Old*

MOHINI, *university educated Development Project worker, 24*

NEESHA, *Mohini's older sister, 26*

CHARU, *Asha's mother, 40 plus*

HAWKER

The action takes place on and around a Delhi construction site. In a corner of Mohini and Neesha's sitting room. On an isolated road in Rajasthan.

ACT ONE

A noisy building site in Delhi in intense heat. Shortly before the mid day break. Scaffolding, reinforcing rods and a partly completed entrance plaza suggest we are on a major site. The cement mixer turns noisily. The CONTRACTOR *holding a glass of hot tea watches as the Rajasthani* WORKERS *head load with wet concrete in baskets and take it up the scaffolding. The* JAMADAR *stands alongside and then busies himself inspecting the work. He is then obscured behind a pile of bricks. The* WOMEN WORKERS *shout to each other but at first we cannot make out what they are saying. The* CONTRACTOR *sips his tea. He now turns towards the site 'office'. On his approach he glances towards a pile of bricks where a* WOMAN *finishes suckling a baby. She puts the baby into one of several ragged hammocks made out of scarves and suspended between rods and then picks up her head loading basket and joins the other workers. The sound of the crying baby now adds to the cacophony. The* CONTRACTOR *passes the 'creche area' where* LALLI *plays in the rubble. He peers into one of the hammocks made of ragged scarves and pushes it causing it to rock and then returns to his office. The cement mixer slows and we begin to make out the dialogue between the women as they pass each other with their loads.*

PARVATI. My head is splitting.

KAMLA. My feet are swelling.

PARVATI. A full month I'm bleeding.

ASHA (*who is heavily pregnant*). My back is breaking.

DADI. The sun is killing.

LALLI. (*who is rocking baby hammocks*). The children are crying. Crying and messing, Auntie. Messing from their stomachs.

PARVATI. Clean them!

KAMLA. Give them water.

DADI. The Thekedar is drinking chai.

PARVATI. Long may it choke him.

DADI (*playfully*). Thekedar, ask me to drink tea with you.

ASHA. It's pay day tomorrow. We'll get our money.

KAMLA. On B site they've finished working.

PARVATI. Where is the Jamadar?

KAMLA. Jamadar! Let us hear the siren. It's time to stop working.

DADI. The sun is killing.

As she passes an oil drum she hits it with a metal bar.

Let us hear the siren.

ASHA. My back is breaking.

KAMLA. Let us hear the siren. (*Ironically.*) Jamadar Sahib! (*Making a crude sign.*) You are our protector! Come to our rescue! Play us your khanjari! (*Tambourine.*)

The JAMADAR appears. He now inspects the contents of the cement mixer, glances at his watch. It is not time yet. The CONTRACTOR stands in the office doorway to beckon the JAMADAR inside.

CONTRACTOR. Jamadar! Come!

The WOMEN continue working. Our attention is now centred on the Jamadar's office. Here the CONTRACTOR is arriving at a decision.

CONTRACTOR. You say you can supply me?

JAMADAR. I can supply.

CONTRACTOR. I'm talking twenty, thirty force head loading.

JAMADAR. Thekedar you have my word.

CONTRACTOR. We are tendering all the time now. We have in our sights 200 kilometres of prime highway, the Inter Stars Hotel luxury complex – big swimming pool, roof gardens, underground parking, four restaurants, the lot. There's a packet of Government work in the pipeline. We can't keep up with the paperwork.

JAMADAR. It's very good.

CONTRACTOR. It's excellent. The economy disintegrates but construction, it's like corruption, always booming, the more you feed it, the hungrier it becomes. I'm talking big bubbles to you my friend.

JAMADAR. I can supply.

CONTRACTOR. I know you can Jamadar. But this is the problem: you must supply at my price. I pay by the job but I want quality work, which is why I come to you. The last guy brought me too many Biharis and U.P.ites. They crib and yak too much. Nothing but aggro.

JAMADAR. My people are different. Happy workers.

CONTRACTOR. Agreed: Rajasthani muzdoors are naturals.

JAMADAR. Very happy workers.

CONTRACTOR. Like camels. They can keep going on nothing. I love them.

JAMADAR. I am a Rajasthani. I bring you only Rajasthani.

CONTRACTOR. That's what I want to hear. I will want your muzdoors on standby. And very soon. There are penalty clauses with all these contracts. I have to be sure.

JAMADAR (*a small note of hesitation*). I can supply. As many as you want. I can get them. I have connections in many villages: Sikar. Deorala. Jhunjhunu. Mundoti. I know them all.

CONTRACTOR. Then it's agreed.

JAMADAR. I can supply, guaranteed . . . as long as the rains continue to fail.

CONTRACTOR. They have failed so far.

JAMADAR. If the rains break these people will scuttle back to their land like children to their mother. Nothing will detain them. As soon as the rains arrive, they flee.

CONTRACTOR Yes, yes, yes, this we know.

JAMADAR. They must go back to work their land. To plant up their crops. Some are already there preparing the soil. A rumour of rain and (*Making a sign of flight.*) cheerio Delhi.

CONTRACTOR. And should the rains continue to fail, as I am confident they will, you are sure of supplying me?

JAMADAR. They can't make daal from dust.

CONTRACTOR. I can tell you from the highest authority, the rains will fail again. Definitely. A hundred and one per cent.

JAMADAR. You have had a sign?

CONTRACTOR. Better. Long range satellite weather forecast. What do you make the time Jamadar? Show me.

The JAMADAR *raises his wrist. The* CONTRACTOR *checks it with his own watch. They wait. The* CONTRACTOR *makes a gesture of casual benevolence.*

CONTRACTOR. All right. Let's take a break.

The JAMADAR *works the siren. The* WORKERS *make their way to the jhuggis.*

JAMADAR. Thekedar sahib, it's pay day tomorrow. My muzdoors will be expecting their wages. It's three weeks since they had money.

CONTRACTOR. Three weeks? Do you know how long I have been kept waiting by the Government, by the developers, by the finance institutions for MY money? It runs into months. At the same time our suppliers are at my throat night and day screaming for settlement. I have to juggle so many balls.

JAMADAR. These people need money for food. They are coming to me every day now for loans. Until you pay me. I don't have to give them. The shops refuse them karza. (*Credit.*) They need their wages.

CONTRACTOR. And I'm telling you the whole industry is in perpetual log jam. I give you what I can, what more can I do?

JAMADAR. Tomorrow they will want to be paid. In cash.

CONTRACTOR. So what's the problem? Pay them. Pay them a little to keep them going, they can have the rest another time. They don't need much to subsist. I'll get on to the bank again. I will do what I can.

The CONTRACTOR *and* JAMADAR *leave the office to take their lunch elsewhere. Before they exit the* CONTRACTOR *remembers something.*

10

CONTRACTOR. By the way, some women are coming round from Mobile Creche or some such charity. Middle class spinsters with degrees from Calcutta, Oxford, Harvard and God knows where. Keep them away from the muzdoors.

JAMADAR. All strangers, hawkers or visitors not permitted on site without permit.

CONTRACTOR. No, no. With these girls I'm obliged to extend a measure of hospitality and welcome. Their uncle is some big shot in Government circles. That fellow in home spun with the silver Mercedes. The polo player? You know him.

JAMADAR. (*who clearly doesn't*). Oh yes, yes.

CONTRACTOR. Just keep them from yakking to the muzdoors and organising these conscious raising jamborees. I don't want brats singing 'Jan-Gan-Man' on my sites. We've got enough flack.

JAMADAR. No talking to muzdoors. I can do.

CONTRACTOR. Just tell them Rajasthanis have their own customs in matters of work. Porridge schools, women with moustaches and glasses on their noses we don't require.

JAMADAR. Exactly so, Thekedar . . . exactly so.

The CONTRACTOR *and* JAMADAR *leave. We now focus on the* WOMEN WORKERS *as they rest, snack, drink from pitchers of water.* KAMLA *is feeding her baby.* LALLI *is massaging* DADI*'s back with her feet.* ASHA *is hugging her swollen belly.* PARVATI *as she prepares food watches* ASHA.

PARVATI (*of foetus*). Does he knock on your walls?

ASHA *shakes her head.*

Do you feel him pulling himself down?

ASHA. I just feel heavy. I can't sleep.

PARVATI. Take it a little easier. Walk slower and don't carry so many bricks today.

DADI. When the belly is wider than the breasts, a woman should not carry a full pitcher of water.

PARVATI. Asha is not carrying water pitchers Mother.

DADI. When the buttocks are bigger than the belly a woman should not carry firewood. Nor should she dig in the fields.

PARVATI (*with irony*). No, she starves instead.

ASHA (*to* PARVATI). Mother-in-law, when will I go home to my village to have my baby? It feels like a stone inside me.

PARVATI. Better than nothing inside you. You will go. When the time is right.

ASHA. Will it be soon?

PARVATI. It will be when it will be.

KAMLA. If she gets much bigger it will be too late. Blossom cannot wait for the bee.

PARVATI. This bee is turning into a hornet. Buzzing around our heads from morning to night. Did not Mohan say he will find out the time tables? Is he not trying his best to make necessary enquiries and arrangements? (*To* ASHA.) Why do you fret so?

ASHA. It was promised.

DADI (*ironically*). I was promised tea every day when I came to work here.

KAMLA (*with joking gestures*). What wasn't I promised!

ASHA. Mother is waiting for me. She sent a message: She has a yellow odhni (*scarf*) ready to give to me and there will be ghutti made for the baby.

DADI. That's the tradition. Traditions must be observed.

PARVATI (*to* ASHA). When Mohan has made the arrangements you will go. He will take you to your mother and the rest of us will work on here and manage the best we can until you return. It will be hard but at least we will have some peace on the subject.

DADI. The custom is that EVERYONE should be there to give songs of thanks to God for safe delivery and to join in the general jollities and celebrations.

PARVATI. Celebrations! What is there to celebrate until there is news of rain? In the fields there is not a gawar pod to be found among the thistles and you talk of celebrations.

DADI. I am just talking about tradition. Traditionally this girl should be in her mother's house now. Sweet herbs will have been gathered, the walls whitewashed, special foods prepared –

PARVATI. You are mixing up life with the stories in the cinema. Next she will be expecting a magic carpet to appear and whisk her away to her village to the music of six chikaras and ten dancing girls doing a phoondi! My son is trying his best. Now let us talk of something else.

LALLI (*to* KAMLA). Auntie. Sonia cinema is having a new film.

KAMLA. Have you been loitering in the streets again?

LALLI. No Auntie. I saw it. When I went to ask the ladies in the houses for clean water. I saw it: Two men on ladders were painting a beautiful poster. There's a dancer in a mauve sari and she has gold nail polish on her toes and pink polish on her fingers and a doctor with glasses on is rescuing her from a burning palace. It's Anil Kapoor and Sri Devi.

PARVATI (*of* LALLI). Her husband is going to be very pleased to discover what a bargain he has made. An expert on film stars and nail polish.

LALLI. I wish I was a film star.

KAMLA (*laughs*). You can be a film star, Lalli. You'll find out on your wedding night. In our husband's bed we're all film stars. When it's dark and a man is needful do you think he can tell the difference between his wife and a film star eh?

LALLI. How should I know?

KAMLA. A bee does not need to know the names of the flowers it enters.

PARVATI. What nonsense is she talking now?

DADI. She's just fooling.

KAMLA. In the dark a husband can be a handsome prince with a moustache. Or a millionaire with a silver car. In the dark who knows?

PARVATI. Kamla, be quiet. (*To* LALLI). Did I not tell you to clean the babies, to keep the flies from their faces? What use is a child bride here? She doesn't work. She doesn't help, all she does is eat and dream of film stars.

LALLI. Auntie I did clean the babies. I took them to the stand-pipe. I splashed them in the oil drum. But then they had more diarrhoea.

KAMLA (*to* LALLI). Go, take the babies to the pipe. They are smelling again.

LALLI *leaves the group to take babies off stage.*

PARVATI (*calling after her*) . . . and then find wood for the stove . . . a fire also has to eat something . . .

DADI. They have diarrhoea because the water here is not clean.

KAMLA. They have diarrhoea because people here do their business too close to the jhuggis.

DADI. In the village we don't have these smells. The poison clouds from the traffic and the noise all day. In the village we have clear skies and hear only the sounds we make ourselves.

PARVATI. In the village it's wonderful: you can starve in silence under a beautiful sky.

DADI. Parvati, your tongue has too much acid on it these days.

PARVATI. Soon the siren will start again. There is no rest here night or day. It hurts even to raise your eyes.

KAMLA. Tomorrow is pay day. Let's think about that.

PARVATI. Think about it! There is nothing to think about. Enough to pay some debts, a bag of lentils, a bottle of oil, some leaf vegetables and salt. Bas.

DADI. And tea. I want my tea. And my sugar. Two days thin milk and tea powder you are giving me.

PARVATI. Next week it will be water only. The way things are going. The Jamadar is giving Mohan no work for three days again. What are we to eat?

KAMLA. I'd love a piece of juicy coconut. Something good and fresh to bite on. To get the taste of dust out my mouth.

PARVATI (*to* KAMLA). If you talked a little less, less dust would enter.

DADI. What am I working for? Eight hours a day, the cement seeping into the bones of my head, up and down to the roof.

My neck is cracking with the weight, what am I working for
if I cannot have a little tea? I ask only for somewhere to lie
and a morsel to eat, and my tea. I don't eat much now, my
stomach has shrunk, my teeth are broken. I don't ask a lot,
only my tea . . .

PARVATI. Mother, give our ears a rest. Find a different song.

DADI (*shuffling off*). I only ask for my tea . . .

PARVATI. You will get your tea! If we have to work extra hours
morning into evening, dawn into dusk, flesh into sores, bones
into dust . . . let no one say we deprive our mother of her tea!

DADI. I have nothing. I give everything to my children. I have
nothing but my anklets, soon you shall have them too, when I
am no more use to you.

DADI *gets up and takes her food to sit away from the others
and begins to hum and then sing.*

DADI. My bracelets and my anklets
Two of wood and six of silver
A gift from my husband's people
In their grip I am forever
From the day I was married
A gift from my husband's people.
Two of wood and six of silver
I am valued by my bracelets.
The work in their making
The weight of the silver
By which I am valued
My bracelets and my anklets.
I wear them always
In the fields of my village
In my bed of conception
On the sites of construction
In the gutters of Delhi
I wear them always
My bracelets and my anklets.
Until the night I die
My bracelets and my anklets.
By which I am valued
Will be taken from me.

The others join in the song

A young man will be waiting
A young bride will be chosen
My bracelets will be given
My bracelets and my anklets
Two of wood and six of silver
To the bride who has been chosen
My bracelets will be given
To become the new bride's story
My bracelets and my anklets.

The siren begins its wailing. The WOMEN *prepare to move off to work. The* JAMADAR *approaches.*

JAMADAR. I want to discuss with Mohan.

PARVATI. You have some work for him at last?

JAMADAR. Speak with respect or I'll go find another mistri.

PARVATI. He has gone to the bus station.

JAMADAR. The bus station? The direction he was taking from here this morning was towards the beer hall.

LALLI is returning with the babies. She lifts one from a basket into the scarf hammock. The other she holds and rocks.

ASHA. He has gone to the bus station Jamadar. To enquire for the bus to my village.

JAMADAR. Are you people deaf? Did you not hear the siren or shall I dock your pay? Tell Mohan he can work tomorrow. But I want him fit. No hangovers on this site. Happy workers only here . . . and I want to see him as soon as he comes. About another matter.

The JAMADAR *looks towards* LALLI *before he leaves. The* WOMEN *stand.* KAMLA *takes the baby from* LALLI *and attempts to feed it with gruel. It doesn't want it.*

PARVATI. Kamla!

KAMLA. Too much dust. His eyes are stuck together. Like he is a blind boy.

She uses saliva to clean the baby's eyes.

(*To baby.*) Open your eyes Beta. See the world. He won't open. He doesn't want to live.

ASHA. He cries so much. Come baby, don't cry, why do you cry?

KAMLA. My milk is bad and the water here is stale. There is nothing good for him to take. It comes out black from his bowels. Look at his legs, thin, quivering like a mosquito.

We hear PARVATI *calling again.*

PARVATI. (*offstage*). Kamla . . .

KAMLA (*calling*). Coming! I will lose this one. He's too small and thin.

ASHA. Take him to the clinic for medicine.

KAMLA. How many times I've been there. (*Quoting.*) 'Salt, sugar and water, Mother.' A day of work lost. 'Salt, sugar and water'. But the water here is not good. It tastes of metal.

KAMLA returns the baby to its hammock.

KAMLA. When they're born on the sites they are lost children. The only mother's song this baby hears is the cement mixer, the stone cutting machine shrieking – yee, yee, yee yee, the air he breathes is from the backside of lorries, how can he grow? I will lose this one. But I have three others. It's good that you are going to your mother for your first born.

PARVATI. Kamla!

KAMLA (*calling*). I'm coming. (*To* LALLI.) Lalli, hide your face behind your odhni better when you are outside the jhuggi. Soon you will be a woman. Don't show your face so much.

KAMLA goes to site to work. LALLI *lowers scarf and goes to fetch wood.* PARVATI *watches as* ASHA *straightens up with difficulty.*

PARVATI. Stay in the shade for a while longer.

ASHA. No. I'm rested.

PARVATI. I'll ask Jamadar to give you easier work.

ASHA. Every hour is another four rupees. I must take some mithai for my mother when I go home to have my child. She will expect it.

The siren sounds again.

PARVATI (*to siren*). All right! (*To* ASHA.) If your waters break, travel will not be easy. Rest a little more and then if you find strength you come and work. Rub oil on your stomach, comfort the child inside you. Appease your child.

PARVATI *leaves.* ASHA *takes oil from a small bottle and rubs her belly under her dress.*

ASHA (*to baby*) . . . Are you a boy? I hope you are a boy for Mohan's sake. He wants a son. I want you be a son as well. You'll buy me presents when you're big. You'll ask my opinion about everything. You'll bring me a bride to do my housework and earn money for me. She'll do whatever I tell her. Without arguing. Or sulking. I'll be the boss.

I wouldn't mind that much if you were a girl. I could comb your hair and make it pretty. I could stitch a little dress for you and teach you some songs . . . Oh God, please let me have this baby in my mother's house. Because she is waiting. Because it is my first. And I am frightened! Soon we will ride to my village on the Up Country Janakpuri bus. It is only a day to the village. If we leave early before the sun shows, before the street sleepers wake, we will be there at dusk. My mother will bring a torch to show us the path from the road to our village. It is not so far. A Khejora tree points the way across the sand to our house. We will hear bells from the slumbering camels and dogs barking to greet us. Grip inside me for a little while more. The walls of my mother's house are high and the floors cool. My mother will sing to you. 'La la la, la la la la . . . ' My sisters will tickle your feet with a silken corn tassel and my father he will carry you above his head to show you to all the people. 'La la la, la la la . . . '

MOHAN *arrives.*

ASHA. Mohan!

MOHAN. Give me cool water.

ASHA *pours water from a clay pot into a metal beaker.* MOHAN *drinks.*

MOHAN. You can't work?

ASHA. Your mother said I must rest. For the baby. What did you find out?

MOHAN. No rain in Rajasthan.

ASHA. About the bus.

MOHAN. About the bus?

ASHA. I'm getting so big. Look. You got the tickets?

MOHAN. It's impossible.

ASHA. Oh Mohan!

MOHAN. Every bus is full up.

ASHA. What will we do?

MOHAN. No room.

ASHA. I promised my mother. My mother who I haven't seen since my wedding. My mother who waits for me . . .

MOHAN. There is no room. Always full. No tickets to buy. It's a waste of time to queue.

ASHA. You didn't go. Again you didn't go to do it.

MOHAN. I went. Keep your voice small. I went – to get on the bus, you have to know people. Contacts. I am trying to make necessary contacts.

ASHA. There are lorries, all the time there are lorries going up country. I've seen them, there are trains.

MOHAN. Trains! You have to be a Government official to even queue for the queue for a train. Trains! Stop this weeping. I will get you home.

ASHA. There won't be time. My belly is fully stretched. The child will not wait inside me much longer.

MOHAN. I will try again tomorrow. There is a man who has a nephew with a lorry. Taking metal sheets to Jaipur.

ASHA. To Jaipur?

MOHAN. Are the baby's hands in your ears? From Jaipur there will be other lorries. I will go again tomorrow to make hard and fast arrangements.

A pause.

ASHA. You still have the money?

MOHAN. What money? Give my head a rest.

ASHA. You still have the five hundred rupees? For the journey.

MOHAN. Sure.

ASHA. The jamadar has work for you tomorrow.

MOHAN. And what I'm telling him is what I'm telling you. Tomorrow I am making final arrangements for transportation to your village. Your first child will be born in your mother's house. It's the custom. The Jamadar knows that.

ASHA. I feel happy again. We will go soon, won't we?

MOHAN (*gently*). It's my duty. Have I failed my duty to you in other respects? Have I not given you a child?

ASHA. Yes.

MOHAN. Do I beat you?

ASHA. You don't beat me.

MOHAN. Do you cry with hunger? Do you search the gutters for food like the beggars? Do you sleep on the railway sidings? Are you molested by strangers? Have I not behaved to you as a husband?

ASHA. You have.

MOHAN. So I never want to feel your anger again. To smell your suspicions. Do you understand me, Asha?

ASHA. Yes.

MOHAN. And find your smile. It's pay day tomorrow. We will get to your village whatever it costs.

ASHA. Mohan, the Sikh in the dukan has a glass bowl for dahi (*yoghurt*). It would be a nice gift to take for my mother.

MOHAN. Glass breaks.

ASHA. He will wrap it well. He will give it to me for only 40 rupees. It is green like mint. Very pretty. And it has a pattern of diamonds round the edge. Only 40 rupees. Little more than a day's work. And I'm working extra this week. I'll do another shift now. It will be nice, won't it? To take something to give my mother when we arrive in my village.

MOHAN. It will be nice.

ASHA. I feel so happy now.

ASHA *goes to join the other* WORKERS.

MOHAN (*to himself, he's very worried*). It will be a bloody miracle.

From his pocket MOHAN *takes a liquor bottle, unscrews it, takes a swig before making for his bed behind the cloth door of the jhuggi. The focus is now on the site where the women are working.*

PARVATI (*to* ASHA). Has he come?

ASHA. He has come.

PARVATI. Does he have the tickets?

ASHA. Tomorrow, he will have them.

KAMLA (*she is reporting on below*). Fine ladies are now going from B site to D site.

PARVATI. How do they look?

KAMLA. Like all the others. Miserable.

PARVATI. Wearing dark glasses?

KAMLA. Dark glasses and handbags.

KAMLA (*to* ASHA). The tickets are bought?

ASHA. Tomorrow. Tomorrow for sure.

KAMLA. Tomorrow is the robber of our lives. I don't trust tomorrow.

PARVATI. If a wife cannot trust her husband what use has she for tomorrow? She might as well commit sati on her wedding night. (*To* ASHA.) If my son has told you the child is to be born in your mother's house, so it will be.

Our attention is again on the jhuggis where the JAMADAR *carrying a heavy box puts it down and opens the curtain of* MOHAN'*s door.* LALLI *watches from close by. She's holding a baby.*

JAMADAR. Mohan! Come out you fool. Mohan! (*To* LALLI.) Why aren't you working? Eh? Can't you speak? Why aren't you working?

LALLI. I'm not old enough.

JAMADAR. Not old enough? How old are you then?

LALLI. I don't know.

JAMADAR. You look old enough to me. Here . . . take it . . . take it.

He throws her a toffee. LALLI *takes it.*

Don't be frightened. Mohan!

MOHAN *comes out of jhuggi.*

JAMADAR (*kicking box*). Why are you wasting my time? It doesn't work.

MOHAN. No, no, it works. It's a hundred per cent working model. Star satellite, four channel. Guaranteed.

JAMADAR. What did you pay?

MOHAN. I saw it working. It's the same one. It's guaranteed. When he showed it to me it was working. Zee TV. Beautiful picture.

JAMADAR. How much did he take from you?

MOHAN *doesn't want to say.*

MOHAN (*to* LALLI). Beat it!

LALLI *moves off a little distance.*

JAMADAR. Face it. You've been done. I got the mechanic to take a look. It doesn't work. It's useless.

MOHAN. Maybe in the journey – a little knock. Something was disturbed – it's nothing.

JAMADAR. I'm telling you again, IT DOESN'T WORK!

MOHAN. It can be mended.

JAMADAR. There is nothing in it to mend. You borrowed my money. I want it back. You have been tricked.

MOHAN. I swear by my life it was working. By my unborn child's life. It was perfect.

JAMADAR. Maybe. But now most of the essential parts are missing. They are no longer there. They have been removed. Take a look.

MOHAN. I don't want to look.

JAMADAR. How are you going to pay me back?

MOHAN. It was working perfect. One touch selection.

JAMADAR. I asked you a question, how are you going to pay me?

MOHAN. How am I going to pay the money lender? I'll find the man who sold it to me. I will get the money back.

JAMADAR. Your arse is where your head should be, you fool. Why don't you stick to what you can do? Accept your dharma instead of coming up with these wild ideas. Remember your box of ladies shoes. Two gross of them you bought. Assorted Ladies Shoes. You took two hundred rupees from me for down payment. They are still sitting in my house under lock and key. I'm hiding them from my wife. Not one shoe is like another. Not one right foot matching a left foot. Not one. My wife is thinking there is something shameful I'm hiding. All because I tried to help you.

MOHAN. I'll pay you back. I'll work hard. Give me a chance Jamadar. It was a brilliant idea.

JAMADAR. I don't want to listen to you. You with your brilliant ideas. Come to me ever again with your brilliance and I'll make your head look like a split pomegranate.

He kicks MOHAN.

MOHAN. Is it a crime to try and improve your lot?

JAMADAR. It's a crime to borrow money without returning it. The money lender will soon be sending his gang after you. You'd better sort something out fast.

A WOMAN WORKER *calls 'Jamadar. Jamadar, come' and beckons. The* JAMADAR *kicks* MOHAN *again and then walks away.* MOHAN *rubs his bruises and then opens the cardboard box and takes out a TV set and turns the knobs. He becomes aware that* LALLI *is watching.*

MOHAN. What are you gawping at?

LALLI. Is it a TV uncle?

MOHAN. No, it's a cow with ten tails.

LALLI. Can't you make it work uncle?

MOHAN. If I could make it work I would be a rich man. People would come to my jhuggi and watch whatever they liked. For a few coins only. Newsreel. Festivities. BBC, prayers. Cricket – The World Cup. India might be winning – that was my dream.

LALLI. Can it show films?

MOHAN. If it was working it would show many films. All the muzdoors would pay to see them. Day and night they would be watching. Beautiful colourful programmes.

LALLI. Would it show Anil Kapoor? Would it show costumes and dancing? And songs and feasts and lovely furniture?

MOHAN. Everything you want to see, it can show. It would show us a better life. If it was working.

LALLI. Can't you make it work so we can see the pictures?

MOHAN. It is silent. It shows nothing. I have been cheated. Nothing.

MOHAN stares at the TV set. LALLI sits next to him and also stares at the screen. Sounds of babies crying. Sound of cement mixer and general site noise heightens. In the JAMADAR's office the CONTRACTOR leads in MOHINI and NEESHA. Oxford educated sisters.

CONTRACTOR. Come, come. Take a seat. I have sent for refreshments. I trust you girls are not too dusty.

MOHINI. We're absolutely fine. Thank you.

CONTRACTOR. I know your uncle well. Known him since our days at college. We catch up with each other now and again. He said you girls were interested in the muzdoors. Of course I already knew that you were involved in this kind of thing. There was a programme on TV about your venture. Sisters of Hope, isn't it?

MOHINI (*correcting him*). The Rural Sisterhood Project. RSP.

CONTRACTOR. My wife was most taken by the work you people are doing with the desperate and dying.

MOHINI. Actually we're more involved with the struggles of the living.

CONTRACTOR. So moving and colourful. We're not used to seeing such attractive girls doing this kind of work. Sister Theresa and her camp are hardly Miss World candidates. I trust I've been of some assistance to you.

MOHINI. You have, thank you. You've been most generous with your time.

CONTRACTOR. And you can put me down definitely for your fund raising gala ball shindig. Give me six tickets.

MOHINI. That's great.

CONTRACTOR. I gather you're laying on lashings of celebrities. Exactly who is coming?

NEESHA (*sarcastic*). Prince Charles.

MOHINI. We've been promised lots of support from so many kind people.

She tears out tickets from book.

CONTRACTOR. My wife by the way is a Royal Family fan. She collects Princess Di.

NEESHA *gets up to look out of window.*

I wouldn't dare to arrive home without the ball tickets. And of course her sisters in law would never forgive her if they weren't included too. Make it eight.

MOHINI. That's most generous. Thank you so much.

CONTRACTOR. I know your uncle will be attending. As a matter of fact when he phoned me about your visit here he was quite emphatic. 'A.J., whether or not you care for dancing and all that kind of palaver is not the issue, buy the damn tickets or I'll never hear the end of it from those nieces of mine.' Your uncle and I are buddies from way back you see.

NEESHA. I need some air.

MOHINI *and the* CONTRACTOR *are thrown.*

CONTRACTOR . . . buddies from way back.

NEESHA (*to* CONTRACTOR, *cool, as a matter of information*) I practically stepped on a new born baby. It was on a piece of rag a few inches away from the cement mixer. A week old baby left on the ground while its mother was humping cement.

CONTRACTOR. It should not have been placed there. These women are very neglectful. We tell them plenty of times: 'Keep your little ones out of the way.' They're not educated. They're simple people. The drinks will be coming along. If you will kindly sit and relax.

NEESHA. I don't want your drinks.

MOHINI. Neesha! (*to* CONTRACTOR.) Actually what we wanted to ask –

NEESHA. Ask him why he doesn't have a creche or latrines, or . . . something for these women. (*To* MOHINI.) I'm . . . (*Deciding to go.*) going outside for a bit.

MOHINI. I'll . . . I'll catch you up. I'll see you in the car.

NEESHA *leaves.*

MOHINI. My sister suffers terribly from migraines.

CONTRACTOR. That's most regrettable. Most unfortunate.

The JAMADAR *enters with cold drinks and snacks and places them on table and leaves.*

MOHINI. I do apologise.

CONTRACTOR (*stung*). No need, no need. It's cute. You girls gad about freely abroad to Europe, Australasia and the States, Norway, Holland and every ruddy where for a couple of years. The Third World is such a fashionable subject for study in these places. And then you return to teach us how to manage our poverty.

MOHINI. We're not like that. I assure you.

CONTRACTOR. You know, we have our very own home grown indigenous development and poverty industry banging us on the head daily with radical ideas and solutions. From fundamentalists to environmentalists, nutritionists to Green-peacers: grow more trees, sink more wells, save the worm, save the world. We are polluted with saviours. Both imported and home grown.

MOHINI. Please understand ours is not essentially a political movement.

CONTRACTOR. You want to ease the burden of these women? Why?

MOHINI. Everyone recognises that Modern India has been built on their backs, surely they deserve a little more?

CONTRACTOR. Do you know what these people are really good at, experts at, these muzdoors you want to lionise? Poverty. I'm not jesting. They are experts at being poor. This incidentally is the greatest achievement of the majority of our people. We have refined ways of coping with adversity. India has been going a long time. We are supreme survivors.

MOHINI. Perhaps survival isn't quite enough any more.

CONTRACTOR. Look, our family have been in this business since before the Raj, we know most of the questions. Now, tell me what do you imagine is the primary fear of these muzdoors? Hunger, disease, war?

MOHINI. I wouldn't presume.

CONTRACTOR. I watched you and your sister looking so aghast while the muzdoors carried the cement to the roof, the water in skins on their back, up and down in the heat. I could read your minds perfectly well. Why don't they use a hoist? Why don't they supply a pump, a lift, a ramp, a drill, a crane? Mechanisation, your dream for these people, it brings terror to their hearts. The muzdoors are cheap labour, dirt cheap you might say, and they prefer to stay cheap. Why? They haven't had the benefit of an Oxford University education but even the most simple of them knows this: the day they are not cost effective, the machines take their place on the sites. And then where will they be? You see. India is a very poor and complex country. For every solution you come up with, two and a half more problems arise.

MOHINI *stands. A HAWKER with bicycle cart arrives at another part of the stage and sets up his stand.*

CONTRACTOR (*a lighter, playful, recovered mood change*). But don't be disheartened. There is always room in this country for pretty young saviours. Now how many tickets to your ball would I have to buy to ensure a dance with you?

MOHINI (*gamely*). As many as you can afford.

The CONTRACTOR *writes a cheque.*

CONTRACTOR. You're definitely promising me a dance?

MOHINI. I'll dance with anyone if it helps our project.

MOHINI *places the cheque in her bag and smiles beautifully as she shakes hands with the* CONTRACTOR.

The CONTRACTOR *smiles. Sees* MOHINI *out.* MOHAN *with his TV enters and stops.*

HAWKER. Did you find your man?

MOHAN. He is not to be found today.

HAWKER (*of TV*). Still not working?

MOHAN. Some parts are working.

HAWKER. You can't find other parts?

MOHAN. I don't have money. All my money is in this machine. I must find the man. It was working before. He must make it work again.

The HAWKER *calls out to advertise his wares: 'Limcas! Cold drinks!'*

MOHAN (*to* HAWKER, *offering small coin.*) Give me news.

The HAWKER *takes a soiled looking newspaper from inside his jacket.*

HAWKER. What news do you wish?

MOHAN. My stars. I was born on the night of Diwali.

HAWKER. What prediction do you want? Life. Romance. Money. Health. Lucky Numbers. Perfect Partner . . . Career Prospects . . .

MOHAN. Money.

HAWKER. Born on Diwali, financial prospects: think before you dive. Your health needs attention. A journey is on the cards. Lucky number 6. Lucky colour green.

MOHAN. Nothing else? That's all?

HAWKER. What do want for a rupee? Ten books on the subject!

MOHAN. Give me the weather forecast.

HAWKER. The weather forecast? Where? Here. Delhi?

MOHAN. Rajasthan. Is there rain coming?

HAWKER (*finding page, reading*). Rajasthan and U.P. 'Aridity continues . . . hot and dry'.

The HAWKER *spots something as he turns over page.*

HAWKER. But look, see, in Mundoti there was a cloudburst.

MOHAN. In Mundoti? When?

HAWKER. This is today's newspaper. 'In Mundoti a cloudburst was reported. One bullock slipped and broke its leg, much housing affected. The Minister of Ag' – this is why they are reporting it, a big gun is visiting ' – on a fact finding mission'.

MOHAN. How long did the rain last?

HAWKER. This article is not concerning itself about rain in every little village, it's about the minister and his fact finding mission.

MOHAN. But you say there was rain.

HAWKER. I don't say, the newspaper says.

MOHAN *curses in Hindi picks up the TV and moves off stage.*

HAWKER (*calling after him*). If you want up to the minute intricate meteorological details, get yourself a TV that works!

The focus now centres on the site where NEESHA *is watching* DADI *shovel gravel.*

NEESHA. Tell me, what do you women do in your spare time?

KAMLA (*ironically*). Dancing.

NEESHA. You like to dance?

KAMLA. Yes. We are good dancers.

NEESHA. And you have the time to dance?

KAMLA. What do you think!

DADI (*as a matter of information*). When somebody is married, or someone is born we find time to dance. When we have news of rain we will return to our village and then it's different. Then we really dance. The children, the old, the crippled, the blind, the birds, the dogs, everybody dances to welcome the new rain.

NEESHA. That should be happening soon shouldn't it?

KAMLA. Ask the sky.

NEESHA. Your feet are bleeding.

KAMLA. The stones are sharp.

NEESHA. Have you women visited our development projects? We've got a couple going in your area.

DADI *giggles*.

Have you? What's funny, eh? What's amusing you so much? What is she laughing at?

DADI. Evening bags.

NEESHA. What? What is it you're saying?

KAMLA. We've been to projects.

NEESHA. Yes? And did you learn anything?

KAMLA *and* DADI *laugh together*.

NEESHA. Nothing at all?

KAMLA. We learned.

NEESHA. What? Come on, tell me. Reading?

DADI. Yes, reading. 'Name is Dadi. Am Rajasthani.'

NEESHA. Sounds excellent. Very good.

KAMLA. Who can eat reading?

NEESHA. Surely there were other things to learn.

KAMLA. Evening bags!

DADI. Embroidered evening bags! Napkins!

They shout it several times and laugh exuberantly. It's a great joke.

KAMLA. Embroidered evening bags! And napkins!

DADI. Table napkins! Embroidered evening bags.

CONTRACTOR (*calling from distance*). Excuse me Madam, is everything all right?

NEESHA (*to* CONTRACTOR). Yes. Thank you. (*To WOMEN.*) I'm sure we will see each other again.

DADI *and* PARVATI *make signs of farewell.* NEESHA *exits.*

DADI. They smell so sweet these city women. Their hands are fine and smooth. Their feet are pretty.

KAMLA. We all shit in the same way.

As the women continue shovelling and filling the sacks.

KAMLA. Those evening bags! The little beads we had to thread. One mistake. Reject. No good. Unpick. Start again. Perfect or Reject. Nothing between. Those small small needles. These city people like everything to be the same.

DADI. The same but not for long. They order maroon. No other colour we use is any good. Throw it away. Maroon is the colour they are all crying for. Maroon, maroon! We make everything maroon. Scarves, tableclothes, bedspreads . . . We hate to work just with one colour but we must follow the desires of the rich. Two months later the work is returned. No good. Maroon is out now. Not in fashion. Now it's purple. Between purple and maroon there is not much difference. But they will not have it. Our work sits unsold. So many maroon tablenapkins! Evening bags and table napkins.

KAMLA. And we were dying by the day. There was not a tree in leaf. Even the camels were crying. The village well was dry and they were bringing in water by road. There was no milk in the animals, no food in the fields. The young boys were sent to find work in the brick kilns of Delhi and Farida-bad, many men went to sugar factories in Punjab, my cousins went to Iraq, some to Iran, we didn't see them for three years. Everybody was running away from the big drought.

DADI. I lost two children in that time.

KAMLA. Then one day the Ramseva walla came with his sun umbrella and a big folder to tell us the news. People with education had come to save us. (*To audience.*) To teach us how to make –

DADI. Evening bags!

KAMLA. Evening bags and table napkins. How many hours did we walk in the heat to this place where they were going to save us. Powdered milk and lessons. Self sufficiency and solidarity. How to make napkins for people in cold countries who have so much to eat there is still food around their mouths and on their hands when they are finished.

Sound of babies crying.

My little Mungi had not a covering to shield her and I was sewing beads in small stitches into the night until my eyes were falling out. Evening bags and table napkins. One morning a woman from Bombay came to teach us how to use new design stoves. We sat on the ground listening politely to this woman in a silk sari, her hair oiled and her cheeks plump. We sat on the ground our lips cracked, our babies sucking air. She demonstrated a vegetable daal. We had no vegetables, but we came every day. We were very attentive. She was so beautiful. Her voice was soft, her eyes so shining. We had nothing to cook on these stoves. But we came every day to look at her face and listen to her musical voice. She was like a goddess. Now we have the cinema.

LALLI *calls from the creche area.*

LALLI. Auntie! Auntie!

DADI. What?

LALLI. Baby's crying.

DADI. Put something in its mouth! A piece of roti! Your finger. Parvati! Parvati!

LALLI. Baby is still crying! His stomach is emptying everywhere.

DADI. I'll go. Parvati! O Parvati!

KAMLA (*to audience*). That year it was so dry fires started without reason. A tree in its anger would decide to burn itself out. As if it had stopped believing in rain. It tried everything to survive. Trees are very patient. First it dropped its fruit, then it shed its leaves, then it cracked its bark. It waited. The ants sheltered in the cracks turning its sap into running sores. Yet still believing in its own survival, next the tree gave up its smaller branches. The birds flew away from it, the ants entered it more deeply and still it stood waiting for the rain which had given it birth. One season, two seasons, its roots gripped the earth in the hope of rain.

NEESHA *appears again, sits on half finished steps.*

And one day, just like that, without warning (*She makes a sudden clapping action.*) it exploded into fire.

The JAMADAR *approaches.*

It burnt for a whole day and night, a fierce red light and the sparks were big and bright and set fire to other dying trees and smaller bushes and thorns. And in the morning the rains came.

JAMADAR. Am I paying you to work with your tongue?

KAMLA. We have almost finished our quota.

JAMADAR. Take your shovel to B site. The gravel is to be shifted today.

KAMLA. B site is not our quota.

JAMADAR. Don't give me lafda. (*aggravation.*) If it's not shifted today then I'm in trouble. And if I am in trouble who will give you work? Shift the gravel and then we can all rest.

KAMLA (*calling as she goes off*). Parvati! Dadi! Asha!

The JAMADAR *inspects the cement mixer and then exits.* MOHINI *now appears. She's been searching for* NEESHA.

MOHINI. I've been waiting by the car.

NEESHA. There was no need for you to wait.

MOHINI. What are you doing here anyway? We've got a million and one things to chase up.

NEESHA. Take the car and . . . (*Makes a gesture.*) . . . chase them.

MOHINI. What is wrong with you today Neesha?

NEESHA *seems unable to say.*

MOHINI. Let's get home shall we?

NEESHA (*mimicking*). Shall we?

MOHINI. Listen Neesha I've just about had enough.

NEESHA. YOU'VE had enough!

MOHINI. What is going on? Why are you behaving like this?
You've been a ratbag all day.

NEESHA. Mo. I want out.

MOHINI. Out?

NEESHA. I've had it. Out.

MOHINI. Out of what? The Ball? Well that's bloody fantastic.
Ten days to go and you want to pull out. We've still to
finalise the music, the programme notes. The lighting, the
speeches – there are important decisions to be taken and
tonight you know I'm flying to Brussels. Neesha I can't do it
all alone.

NEESHA. I know that –

MOHINI. Someone has to see the accountants, someone has to
meet the VIP's at the airport.

She slaps her neck. A mosquito is hovering.

NEESHA. Mo. I'm no longer interested –

MOHINI (*as if she hasn't heard*). Neesha. I know, the
socialising bit isn't your scene and I'm not asking you to
exchange banalities with beauty parlour princesses or to waltz
with men with gold teeth –

NEESHA (*screaming it*). Will you stop! Stop! Just stop it.

A pause.

MOHINI. OK. Neesh. OK. Shall we go home now, continue our
discussion there?

NEESHA *doesn't respond.*

This is hardly the place to squabble. I'm getting bitten to
death. I can't take much more of these mosquitoes. And I've
a million and one things to do. If you've started a headache
the best thing is get home and lie down in the dark. Shall we
go now?

NEESHA (*turning away*). You go.

MOHINI (*a pause*). OK. If that's what you want. I'll go.

> MOHINI *exits. Lights dim to Early Evening.* NEESHA *sits
> very still. The* HAWKER *begins moving off calling out
> 'Limcas. Cold drinks . . . '*

NEESHA (*to* HAWKER). Where is the bus stop?

HAWKER. Taxi rank over there. (*Points.*) Rickshaw and Scooter
rank further, further.

NEESHA. The bus stop. Where is the bus stop?

HAWKER. Bus office is not close by. Take a taxi. Taxi rank is
over there, not far.

NEESHA. I want the bus. If you'll kindly point me in the right
direction. Thank you.

> NEESHA *follows the direction of his arm and exits. The*
> HAWKER *turns to audience.*

HAWKER. Buses is not for ladies like her. Too much crushing
and shoving. Buses are full of odorous people. Too many
bodies pressing to get on, pressing to get off. The buses are
always broken because they are always overloaded. Too many
people, not enough buses. Everybody wants to get to their
destination. There is always such a squash. Every day there
are accidents, somebody falls and dies. Still people chase the
bus and cling on. What is their choice? India is a very poor
country.

> HAWKER *goes off calling 'Limcas. Cold drinks . . .
> refreshments!'*

End of Act One.

ACT TWO

It is now evening and we are focused on the jhuggis. The evening meal is in preparation. PARVATI and DADI are cooking over a small stove. KAMLA is feeding her baby. LALLI is painting ASHA's toenails.

LALLI. This is my favourite colour: maroon.

DADI. Then keep it away from me. (*Jokingly.*) Maybe Parvati would like it.

PARVATI (*to* DADI). And maybe you would like a pinch of pepper in your tea!

KAMLA. Lalli do my feet when you've finished. My husband used to say my feet were my best feature.

PARVATI. The same can be said of a camel.

KAMLA and DADI laugh.

KAMLA. Those two girls today. They have such a way of walking. As if they were being pulled by a rope. And why aren't they married? You'd think a man can be found to take them. They look rich and they are not ugly.

PARVATI. Girls like that they don't have to marry. Nobody can force them. They do what they like.

DADI. They are children.

PARVATI. Children! The older one has a wrinkle!

DADI. The richer you are the longer you can remain a child. But sooner or later even those girls will have to part with their childhood.

KAMLA. Lalli do my toes now.

LALLI. There is only a little left and I won't have enough.

KAMLA (*disappointed*). Oh! And I really like that colour.

ASHA. It's pay day tomorrow. We'll get some more.

36

PARVATI. We're not wasting money again on nail polish. It doesn't last.

LALLI. It gets scratched by the stones.

PARVATI. We have other things to spend our money on.

DADI. I haven't had good tea for three days now.

PARVATI. There will be money for your tea. But this month we also need extra money for Asha's journey. There is zarurat (*need*) from every direction. The money we borrowed to marry Mohan it has to be found. The rains may come any day, where is our seed coming from? Kamla must buy medicine for the baby.

KAMLA. It doesn't want my milk. My milk is bad. I gave it sugar, salt and water. It doesn't want to take it.

DADI. Rice water. I told you.

PARVATI. As soon as we get paid the baby will be taken to the clinic. Medicine must be bought.

DADI. Rice water was all we had.

PARVATI (*calling*). Mohan!

LALLI. Mohan is talking to the men in the metal shop. He has a TV.

PARVATI. A TV! Don't talk nonsense.

LALLI. I saw it. Honestly. I did.

KAMLA. Yes and what did you see on it, singing and dancing?

LALLI. No. Because it was broken.

PARVATI. It's time she started working, old enough or not, she spends the days dreaming. We're breaking our backs and – look at this wood – she doesn't pay attention to what is important.

DADI. She'll be gone to her husband soon enough and then she'll know what it is to be a woman. Always working. Always tired.

PARVATI. It's not so easy for the men. They get tired too.

DADI. A man might say 'I'm too tired today' and rest. But a woman tired or not, will say 'If I don't do muzdoori what will I give my children to eat in the evening?' From the day I went to my husband's family I was always tired. I'd wake at four, grind flour for two hours. At five I'd walk to fetch a couple of pitchers of water. I come back, feed the family and then without having anything myself to eat – put the child on my back and set off to work.

PARVATI (*mockingly*). Those were the days!

DADI. And still I liked to put on sindoor (*vermilion*) and a bright odhni. Why should we look ugly when we work? Dark plum was my colour. Sometimes bright pink, when I was in a naughty mood.

She pats LALLI *affectionately*.

(*Confidential tone.*) Your Auntie Parvati is suffering. Her insides are bleeding again. Too much carrying heavy stones. (*Normal voice.*) I like this polish you have chosen, it's very pretty and bright.

LALLI. It's like red sweets. They're my best sweets, red sweets. (*To* ASHA.) What sweets do you like best Asha?

PARVATI. Only small children and old women need sweets.

ASHA. I like almond sweets. Soft ones.

DADI. Sour sweets are good for stopping hunger.

LALLI. The Jamadar gave me a nice sweet. A toffee.

Everyone stops to take in this information. KAMLA *stands and pushes* LALLI *roughly.*

PARVATI. She should be working. This is what happens.

DADI. The Jamadar! That goat!

KAMLA (*striking* LALLI *a blow with the flat of her hand*). There is only one person to buy you sweets. Your husband.

LALLI. It was only one sweet he gave me!

KAMLA. Your husband, he'll bring you plenty of sweets when the time comes for him to claim you.

PARVATI. The sooner the better. We should send him a message. 'Come and take your bride away. Let her be your worry.' He should come and claim her soon.

LALLI (*starts crying*). I don't want to go to my husband yet!
I don't want to go. Don't send me yet. I'll be good.

DADI. These days, it's easy. People are not so strict with new
brides. Many mothers know if they don't treat a new bride
like their own daughter she will take their son and go. (*To
LALLI.*) You have nothing to cry about. I was married to my
husband when I was two. Like you I knew nothing about
him. They told me he would give me heavy bangles with a
nice design – and anklets – look. (*She polishes them.*) They
didn't tell me he only had one tooth and that his back was
bent and his hands as rough as a vulture's claws! He worked
eight months on the roads in Jammu to earn my silver. He
gave me sweets. And I gave him eight children, five living
and three of them sons. He was hard because his life was
hard. His mother was a hard woman too. From the day I
came into her house she said I was lazy. I walked five miles
to fetch water even before she was awake – and I was lazy.
In the heat I built mud walls in the field to bring water to the
millet – and I was lazy. Only the scraps she gave me to eat.
When the sun was ablaze and I carried dung on my head to
keep the cooking stoves hot, I was lazy. But in the end, she
loved me. It's true. In the end when she was failing she gave
me her hand and she said 'Sita (*Dadi's real name.*) you have
been like a true daughter to me'. It was tradition and custom
that made her hard. In her heart she loved me.

LALLI *is still sniffing.*

DADI. It's right you should cry a little. But only a little. And
we'll all cry with you when the day comes for you to go to
your husband . . . It will be beautiful. We'll follow the cart
from the village to the bus stop, all of us, your sisters, your
friends, your mother, your aunts, all will be crying.

She sings.

Even the sky will sigh when you are gone.
Even the dust will miss you
Even the babool thorn will cry for you
When you are gone

KAMLA *and* PARVATI *and then* ASHA *join in the song*

Bridegroom please come back soon
We beg you bring back our Lalli

Our precious girl. Our dearest dove
Delicious food awaits you
Bring your bride back to the village
The bed will be ready for you
You can spend the night together
Bring her back soon
Bring her back soon
The room will be fragrant
A mirror will be there
And you can look
And see that you are smiling

Finally LALLI *also joins in the chorus.* MOHAN *appears.*

MOHAN. What's all this tamasha about?

PARVATI. Food is ready. What is it I'm hearing about a TV?

MOHAN *shoots* LALLI *a glance.*

MOHAN (*to* PARVATI). Do I sit in your ear? You tell me.

PARVATI. We can't afford any more debt.

She hands MOHAN *a plate of food.*

Where is this TV?

MOHAN. Don't concern yourself about it Mother.

DADI. He is like his poor father, a daytime dreamer.

KAMLA. Is is true then, you bought a TV? A TV that doesn't work?

MOHAN. It's none of your business. Your husband is in Saudi still not sending money, that's your business.

ASHA. Mohan, is it true?

PARVATI. Let the man eat his food.

She gestures for KAMLA *and* LALLI *to leave.* DADI *follows them. They sit together in the open.* PARVATI *adds more food to* MOHAN'*s plate and then takes some garlic to peel and joins other women.* ASHA *watches* MOHAN *eat.*

MOHAN. I heard something today. There was rain in the area of Mundoti.

ASHA. Mundoti. That's near your mother's village! Have you told her?

MOHAN. It's only a rumour. But still.

ASHA. If it was true!

MOHAN. We'd be on our way tomorrow. Pack up our stuff and head home. Away from the evils of this place.

ASHA. What about me?

MOHAN. It's only a rumour!

ASHA. You made my mother a promise.

MOHAN (*throwing the dish aside, causing it to clatter and the* WOMEN *to turn their heads towards jhuggi*). I've promised to work. I've worked. Lifting bricks crushing stones. Look at me. I came to my manhood only four rains ago and my strength is used up. The work breaks my body and your tears are breaking my sleep. I tried to get out of this and I've been cheated.

ASHA. What about the bus tickets?

MOHAN. Now the moneylender is on my back and will send his men to beat me. And all you worry about is bus tickets.

MOHAN *rushes past* ASHA *causing her to fall.*

ASHA. I promised my mother!

The other WOMEN *go to* ASHA *and take her into jhuggi. Cries of lament 'Eyee'. The lights in the jhuggis dim to black. Sound of modern pop music from a mobile cassette.* DIMPLE, *the Contractor's 35-year-old wife in cool jeans and sweatshirt enters singing along with the music. She's holding a bottle of Limca with a straw from which she occasionally sips. Trailing behind her is the* CONTRACTOR *carrying a cake box, into which he dips.*

DIMPLE. I don't see why we have to come here for something sweet. I can get cakes from Claridges. They have an Austrian chap now. Everybody gets their cakes from him . . . You know I don't care much for this local mithai. It's too heavy.

CONTRACTOR (*he hasn't been listening*). What?

DIMPLE. Who's going to eat it? So much mithai. Honestly!

CONTRACTOR. I'm going to eat it.

He selects another cake and continues to eat.

DIMPLE. You'll spoil your shirt. Why don't you wait till we get to the Volvo? Sit in comfort and eat.

CONTRACTOR. This mithai is bloody wonderful. Take one.

DIMPLE. Too much cholesterol for me. Now what is it you wanted me to see here? Not that I can see anything, it's too dark now.

CONTRACTOR It wasn't dark when I suggested it. If you're going to take four hours in the beauty parlour you should send me a fax.

DIMPLE. A.J., are we having an argument? Or are we going to Doggy's for cards?

CONTRACTOR. You decide, baby.

DIMPLE. Darling I've seen your building many times – don't eat so much mithai, it doesn't help your waistline. I drive past here on my way to Hauz Khas market.

CONTRACTOR. Phase one will be finished within the year. I need a decision from you.

DIMPLE. I'm not absolutely sure.

CONTRACTOR. This is a prime site. There are people queuing up for a chance to live here. I can't reserve it for ever. Do you want it or not?

DIMPLE. If I have anything, I want the Penthouse.

CONTRACTOR. You can have the Penthouse. It's yours.

DIMPLE. And I don't want your tacky Indian tiles. Jennifer got hers from London. Habitat. The colours are different. They don't glare so. And the fittings, don't give me local fittings.

CONTRACTOR. Nothing wrong with local fittings. Actually we export them to Habitat.

DIMPLE. They're not the same.

CONTRACTOR. Have what fittings you like. Fittings are not an issue. Are you saying yes to the Penthouse? This is all I need to establish.

DIMPLE. You know my feelings.

CONTRACTOR. Your feelings waver from day to day. I want to have your thoughts. Even the muzdoors are clear about what they want. They want enough food, they want simple shelter, a few rupees and the rains to come on time and they're happy. I like people who know what they want. Look. Mom and Dad have agreed. Bunker and Rajesh are willing and the girls they definitely want to live centrally, they're just waiting for us to decide.

DIMPLE. I'm getting a headache.

CONTRACTOR. Are you saying yes or are you saying no?

DIMPLE. Why must we go along with this joint family thing? Modern couples are setting up very nicely on their own these days.

CONTRACTOR. Modern couples! You're reading too many women's magazines.

DIMPLE. Sylvia and Bhasker have just moved to their own apartment. If she wants his mother's company, there's a little guest room. Sylvia and Bhasker are very happy being so self contained. You should ask Bhasker about it. You'll see.

CONTRACTOR. I don't need to ask Bhasker anything. How he conducts his domestic affairs is his business. Me. I like the company of my family. So I'm old fashioned. I don't care. The joint family system suits me fine. To have my parents and my brothers and their families under the same roof is a pleasure to me. It's a great system. You women have some- one to gossip with, the children have each other to play with, in case of need we are all there to help each other. Why knock it?

DIMPLE. It's so primitive.

CONTRACTOR. I buy you tickets to the ball. I'm taking you to the States on vacation. I'm eating your pot noodles and you're calling me a primitive!

DIMPLE. Anyway your mother wouldn't be happy in the penthouse. She's accustomed to living at street level.

CONTRACTOR. So the answer is no? This is your final word?

DIMPLE. I don't like all this tradition all the time. We're living in a modern world. There are satellites (*Points.*) up there. We're even getting the Hollywood Oscars direct.

CONTRACTOR. You're talking rubbish, Dimple.

DIMPLE. These ancient customs and traditions are stifling us.

CONTRACTOR. Bullshit. You have a little spat with my mother about the servants or something trivial and hey presto all tradition is useless.

DIMPLE. All I want is to have my own life, in my own space where I can be in charge of my own destiny. Is that asking so much?

CONTRACTOR. Your own destiny? Who do you think you are? Not even the Gods have that luxury. You don't like tradition and customs? You want to get rid of it all?

DIMPLE. I don't say *all*. Why are you being so touchy today? Usually you're so sweet when we step out. Who's been upsetting you?

CONTRACTOR. You women who keep screeching for change –

DIMPLE. What women are you alluding to now?

CONTRACTOR. You should know this: it is tradition and custom that pays for your beauty parlour bills, your children's expensive education. Tradition and custom is what enables you to turn down the luxury of a penthouse suite while the women who carry the stones on their heads to build it have no choice but the jhuggis, so low they can't even stand up in them. But I don't suppose they tell you that in your glossy women's magazines.

The CONTRACTOR *exits.* DIMPLE *follows.*

DIMPLE. A. J., are you going to leave some mithai for Doggy or what?

Dark. A torch searches on the site. It's PARVATI *and* ASHA.

44

PARVATI (*calling*). Mohan! Mohan! Come inside now! Come to your bed! We can't rest until you come inside . . . Mohan . . . Mohan!

ASHA. Mohan, come to your bed, come and rest!

The women's voices peter out as they move across the site and exit. We still hear them calling as a tarpaulin lifts. It's MOHAN with his TV. He hears the voices, but does not move.

MOHAN (*to audience*). It is a brilliant idea. I'm not a fool, and I'm not a dreamer. Sitting in the dark, telling each other the same old ancient stories, that time is over. (*Pointing to tv.*) There's a new story teller and it speaks equally to the rich and the poor. It's selling to them the same toothpaste, the same banks, the same dreams. Muzdoor, Thekedar, priest, beggar, film star. It speaks equally to all. Every person, every nation, it beams down on them equally with wonderful programmes. This storyteller's voice is so magical soon you forget your own mother's voice and she forgets the voices of her ancestors. There are new stories every day. New faces, new voices. Exciting actions. And you don't have to beg for it, you just – (*Recalling it doesn't work.*) one touch control. I've been cheated. The man who sold it to me and promised me these things, he cheated me. He sold me an empty box and ruined my dreams. Now my life and that of my family and unborn child is spoilt. I'll have to find this man and kill him. What else can I do? That is my tragedy and his also.

We hear PARVATI and ASHA (offstage) calling Mohan. MOHAN covers himself with tarpaulin. Classical music. An ornate curtain and floor cushions suggest we are in a tasteful home. MOHINI is working on her papers. NEESHA enters, tired and dusty in the clothes she was wearing on the site. She is carrying a cake box. She drops a kiss on the back of MOHINI's head. NEESHA is about to open the box and then places her hand on it.

NEESHA (*playfully*). Two guesses.

MOHINI. Don't I get a clue?

NEESHA *shakes her head.*

Not even a little one?

NEESHA (*shakes head*). You're too good at these games.

MOHINI (*sniffing*). I have an idea it might be something chocolatey?

Her face moves closer to the box. NEESHA *moves it away.*

NEESHA. Hey!

MOHINI. If I said chocolate, vanilla and something aromatic . . . would I be close?

NEESHA (*abrasively*). Is that one guess?

MOHINI. No! I'm just – what the hell is the matter with you?

NEESHA. Nothing. Except – you always have to have the edge.

MOHINI. You asked me to guess. I'm trying to guess. What edge?

NEESHA. Oh, forget it.

MOHINI. We're playing a stupid guessing game and for no reason you go off at the deep end.

NEESHA (*dully, as she opens the box and roughly places cakes on the plate*). Carrot and Almond. Chocolate Fudge. Which do you want?

MOHINI (*brightly, a final attempt at reconciliation*). I don't mind, they're all delicious.

NEESHA has turned away.

MOHINI. Shall we save them for after dinner?

NEESHA. Whatever.

NEESHA replaces cakes in box. Pause as both play for time to offset the row they know is about to erupt.

MOHINI. So?

NEESHA. I don't know.

MOHINI (*playing for a laugh. Quoting*). 'My wife collects Princess Di'.

They both laugh, breaking the tension a little.

NEESHA Yea.

MOHINI. You look stressed out Neesh. I've been thinking we both need a break. . . . a holiday. A bit of a rest from the work and India. Somewhere less harrowing. D'you know where I'd like to visit? That place in Portugal where we ate grilled sardines on the beach and met those gigantic Aussies with the backpacks. Let's arrange it when I get back from Brussels.

NEESHA. Oh God!

MOHINI. What? What?

NEESHA. I won't be here when you get back.

MOHINI. Do you know what this reminds me of?

NEESHA. I've thought about it Mo.

MOHINI. When you ran away.

NEESHA. I'm not running away.

MOHINI. We were up all night crying and worrying about you, half the police force was out searching and all because of some little stupidity, you accidently dropped one of mom's ear rings down the well. Or was it her necklace?

NEESHA. It was her ring and it wasn't an accident. I did it deliberately.

MOHINI. Yes. I believe we all actually knew that.

NEESHA. Really? No one bothered to inform me.

MOHINI. Well, no. They always preferred to think well of us, to give us the benefit of any doubts.

NEESHA. Mo: for me it's over.

MOHINI. Before you say any more tell me one thing: exactly when did you decide to sabotage our project?

NEESHA (*gently*). Mo, don't!

MOHINI. I simply don't understand why you want to abandon everything we've worked so hard for. I mean, what has changed?

NEESHA. I think . . . I don't believe we're on the right road.

MOHINI. When we started there was no road! We were walking on shifting sands.

NEESHA. Try to hear what I'm saying.

MOHINI. You're feeling disillusioned, you're pessimistic, you're disheartened. We're not moving as fast as we'd like, we make mistakes, but darling just consider what we've achieved, the bits we've got right. Against all the odds. We've battled and at last people are beginning to take us seriously. Neesha we're THERE. We're established. And now we can build with real materials instead of dreams. We've done the hard bit. Why throw all that away? What is the problem?

NEESHA (*very level and with confidence and even humour. She's worked it out and is sorted*). The problem is I don't like where we are, and even less the direction in which we're heading.

MOHINI. All right. We can adjust.

NEESHA. No. We'd have to start again. Knock it all down.

MOHINI. Knock it down.

NEESHA. All of it.

MOHINI. That's crazy. Think how long it has taken us to get this far, to find the finance, the backing, the high profile, the reputation –

NEESHA. Yea. We're really hip. Neesha and Mohini. India's answer to Geldof.

MOHINI. OK. So it helps that we're young and that we can attract an international following.

NEESHA. Glamour people of the world unite!

MOHINI. I'm not taking much more of this shit from you. Not until you can come up with a sane alternative. What do you propose? That we just give up on the problems!

NEESHA (*exasperatingly calm, even bored*). Perhaps that might be best in the long run. Who knows? But I don't see any point in continuing within the existing structures. They don't work except to hijack and distort every good intention. Come on, look around you!

MOHINI. I don't think we can worry about these things. Why not concentrate on what we can deliver? Showing people ways of fending for themselves, of surviving.

NEESHA. Evening bags and table napkins.

MOHINI. To me it seems very simple. Our poor join the modern world – with all its problems, stupidities, injustices and, yes, evils, or they fall into something else: beyond reach. And if that happens it will be too late to be picky about which type of development project is the purest. Don't bale out now Neesha. Stay and help.

NEESHA. I wouldn't be any good to you, Mo, I'm no longer on your side.

MOHINI. I see. A child with limbs like matchsticks stretches out its hand and you want to question the credentials of the benefactor who puts food on its plate? Is that it?

NEESHA. As far as I'm concerned the time of begging is over.

MOHINI (*sarcastic*). Blood and violence, how delicious!

She opens the cake box and takes a piece of cake and eats.

(*Bitterly.*) It's one way of tackling the population problem,. I suppose. What exactly is it you intend to do?

NEESHA. I'm going to the smallest, poorest desert village I can find, to the starting point of these muzdoors' lives and I'll work it out from there. These cakes are divine.

MOHINI goes on eating, but she has to wipe her face. She seems to be crying.

Black to Dawn. We are on the site again. Ghostly movements as women quietly emerge from jhuggis.

KAMLA (*calling in hushed voice*). Lalli. Lalli, come, do you want the men to see us doing our business? Come before the sun shows its face.

DADI. Dogs were howling in my head all night.

PARVATI (*to ASHA*). Did Mohan come to lie beside you?

ASHA. I waited for him. He has not come.

PARVATI. He will come. It is pay day. He must come. (*Feeling ASHA's stomach.*) It has moved down. You should not lift full load today.

KAMLA (*calling LALLI again*). Lalli, do you want your husband to hear that you are lazy?

LALLI *appears, sleepy, her thumb in her mouth.* DADI,
KAMLA *and* LALLI *move off to the open ground behind the
site.*

ASHA (*to* PARVATI). Mother. If my baby arrives today . . .
what will happen?

PARVATI. I have seen the daiyas do their work. I will cut your
cord. I don't have the sharp grass, but I have a knife. I have
rags. But you must try to stop this baby coming so soon.

ASHA. Maybe Mohan is getting the bus tickets and that is why
he did not come.

PARVATI (*leading* ASHA *away to open ground*). When you
squat, don't push hard. Hold on as long as you can.

As ASHA *and* PARVATI *move out of sight* KAMLA *returns
with a pitcher of water. Something catches her eye. It is*
MOHAN *propped up against the office door with a covering
over his body. He has been sleeping there for half the night.*

KAMLA (*calling*). Is that you? Mohan, is that you sleeping
there? Why didn't you come back last night?

MOHAN. I am back. What business is it of yours? I am back,
waiting for the wages.

KAMLA. Asha was crying all night.

MOHAN. Soon she will be crying day and night.

KAMLA. Is Asha to have her baby here?

MOHAN *is unable to answer.*

KAMLA. It will break her mother's heart.

MOHAN. Don't interfere. (*Pause.*) I must get Asha away from
the city before the moneylender comes. I don't know what to
do anymore. There's a scorpion in wait for every step I take.

KAMLA. Maybe there will be news of rain soon. Then we can
leave this poisonous place. (*She sings.*)

The desert waits for our return.
Bajra til and sarson (*millet, sesame, mustard*) will be grown.
The wells will fill for our return.
Deep, cold and sweet . . .

KAMLA *makes her way to the open ground to wash. The light increases. It is morning. The* JAMADAR *sets up a folding table on the site and calculates wages.* MOHAN *stands before him.* PARVATI, KAMLA *and* ASHA *arrive.* PARVATI *gives* MOHAN *a slap across the shoulders to show her displeasure.*

JAMADAR. Sign. Put your mark.

MOHAN (*looking at chitty*). It's wrong. We worked fourteen days, not eight days. (*With a look to* WOMEN.) Fourteen days we worked.

KAMLA. Fourteen days.

PARVATI. Six days carrying bricks, five days rocks, three days gravel and cement.

JAMADAR. Yes, correct. And owing me? Three months owing me advance for travel, advance for medicine (*To* MOHAN.) when you cut your head slipping on the scaffolding, advance for food, still outstanding, and my commission, ten per cent. (*With a glance to* MOHAN.) Plus some items I will not mention now.

KAMLA. You owe us wages.

JAMADAR. I don't owe you anything – you people owe me. (*Counting out notes.*) In addition the Thekedar has not been paying me three weeks now. Sign. I empty my own purse to give you. Take.

MOHAN (*looking at notes*). It's not enough even for food.

ASHA. We need money for the bus. My time has come.

JAMADAR. Take. Next week maybe I can give a little more advance. Maybe I can line up more work to keep you going. Take.

MOHAN. You're cheating us. We've worked hard.

KAMLA. On the roof all day in the heat.

PARVATI. I've been bleeding from the weight of the cement.

JAMADAR. Take or go. Go back to your dry villages and droughts. Go, see what work you can find there.

MOHAN. Jamadar, Sahib. Please. I ask you. My wife must go home to give birth to our child. It's the tradition. Please.

51

JAMADAR. Is it my fault you choose to couple? Did I force you to give her a child? Is she my wife? My sister? My daughter? I give you money for work. Your private life is not my concern.

ASHA. Without money for the bus I cannot go home.

PARVATI. Jamadar we have worked for you many years in many places. We've built roads with you – canals, bridges. Bank of Baroda, American Express.

KAMLA. You are from our desh. You know our customs.

JAMADAR. And it is because of this that I come to you people first every time to give you work. I give you top priority.

MOHAN. I'll take another loan.

JAMADAR. You'll take a kick up your backside.

MOHAN *looks at the money in his hand and after a pause and in silence pockets it and then he spits in the* JAMADAR*'s direction before making his way to the jhuggis.*

PARVATI (*calling after him*). Mohan!

PARVATI *follows* MOHAN *and stands outside the jhuggi he has entered continuing to call him.*

Mohan, this is not the way . . .

DADI *is sitting outside the jhuggi.* ASHA *now joins* PARVATI.

ASHA Mohan!

MOHAN *comes out of the jhuggi in a clean western shirt, combing his hair. He is about to leave.*

PARVATI Where are you going? To the bus station?

DADI. This boy is in trouble. Running away. Leaving us to suffer. He is not going to the bus station. He is going to the city. To get drunk, to buy broken TV sets while we starve . . .

PARVATI (*pulling* MOHAN). What is happening? Are you turning your face away from your mother?

MOHAN. I have to go. Leave me be.

PARVATI. Where? Where is this boy wanting to go? At least leave us some money.

ASHA. Leave money for the bus Mohan . . . for my mother's name, for your sister's honour, for the name of our child waiting to be born, leave money for my journey . . . Mohan!

MOHAN *has torn himself away and runs off.* ASHA *is taken by* DADI *into the jhuggi to rest.*

PARVATI. Run away! Run away! (*She addresses herself/audience.*) Everything is going, everything is changing. All custom and tradition is disappearing. And soon we also will disappear, we women of the dust.

She sings.

Our family, our strongest thread.
Woven by our ancestors
Holding us together
Our strongest thread
Our family, our unity
Holding us together
In famine and in troubles

DADI *comes out to join in the song.*

The thread is getting thinner
The city makes it weaker
Holding us together etc . . .

As they repeat the song, their voices lower and become a background chant. Our attention now focuses on the creche area where KAMLA *is feeding her baby and* LALLI *plays jacks with pieces of stone.*

KAMLA. Lalli have you ever seen a baby being born? Struggling to come into this world?

LALLI. No.

KAMLA. Surely in your mother's house?

LALLI. No. I haven't.

KAMLA. You haven't heard the women screaming as they push to bring the baby out from darkness into light?

LALLI *shakes her head.*

You haven't seen the daiya cut the cord with sharp grass? Hitting the child to make it cry?

LALLI. No, auntie.

KAMLA. And eaten mithai to celebrate the birth?

LALLI. I've eaten mithai. Plenty of times. When babies have been born. Bhua bought mithai when my sister had a boy. She gave me two pieces.

KAMLA. There will be no mithai or celebration for Asha. Poor Asha. Don't you feel sorry for her?

LALLI. Yes.

KAMLA. She's not so much older than you. Only a few years. And she's going to have her baby on the site. Because there is no money for the bus.

LALLI. Mohan took it.

KAMLA. Mohan has been working so hard for two years now. And he has nothing to show for it.

LALLI. He shouldn't take all the money.

KAMLA. At least he didn't go to Saudi, like my husband. At least he stayed to help his family. He has been trying for two years. To earn more than we eat. It doesn't matter how hard we work, there is nothing to spare but tears.

LALLI. Can I go? I have to fetch wood.

KAMLA. Lalli. I'm telling you something important.

LALLI. Aunty said I should do it.

KAMLA. Do you want Asha to have her baby here on this filthy site?

LALLI. No.

KAMLA. Her baby will surely become sick and die. We are a family. We must help each other, isn't that right?

LALLI. Yes.

KAMLA. We must find a way to send Asha on the bus to her mother. We must find a way to get the money.

KAMLA *leades her towards* JAMADAR's *office.*

The focus is now on the JAMADAR's *office. In the back-ground the* WOMEN (PARVATI, DADI, ASHA) *are working.*

54

KAMLA *and* LALLI *arrive near* JAMADAR's *office.*
KAMLA *lowers* LALLI's *scarf and then leaves her by his*
door. The JAMADAR *is stirring his tea when* LALLI *enters*
nervously.

JAMADAR. Come. What do you want? Who sent you?

LALLI. Nobody.

JAMADAR. Nobody? Come. Come closer. Nobody sent you.
You've come to see me. For what reason?

LALLI. I don't know.

JAMADAR. Maybe you've come for a toffee?

He hands her one. She places it down her dress for later.

JAMADAR. What a strange place to put a toffee. Eh?

LALLI. Kamla.

JAMADAR. Kamla?

LALLI. Kamla sent me.

JAMADAR. Kamla sent you. For what purpose? Look, either
tell me what you want or take yourself and your dirty little
face somewhere else. I have other things to attend to.

LALLI (*reciting it*). 'Jamadar please give me money and I will
do dance for you.'

A pause.

JAMADAR. Dance.

LALLI *raises her scarf and performs a pathetic couple of*
steps.

The JAMADAR *hands* LALLI *a coin.*

JAMADAR. Come tomorrow.

LALLI *leaves. Her head covered. We now focus on*
PARVATI, KAMLA, ASHA *by the cement loading bricks*
with pained expressions as if they are subconsciously
covering up and obliterating from their minds what has gone
on in the hut.

MOHAN *now enters and hides behind rubble. He has been*
in a fight and looks dishevelled and frightened. He makes a

hissing sound which PARVATI *recognises. The others continue working.*

PARVATI (*carrying a load of bricks detours to where* MOHAN *lurks*). Who has done this? Come to the jhuggi. I'll wash your head. What has happened?

MOHAN. Mother don't ask questions. Something bad has happened. Take this ticket. Put Asha on the bus.

PARVATI Asha cannot travel alone. Who shall go with her with one ticket? Better she should have her child here. What has happened to your face?

MOHAN. Mother listen to me. Put her on the bus. She will not be travelling alone. I will join the bus some stops out of the city. At Jawalar Junction. At Jawalar Junction I will be joining the bus.

PARVATI. Your head is bleeding. Let me wash it.

MOHAN. If people come. I am not here. Asha is not here. Say nothing. You don't know anything.

PARVATI. What have you done! What will happen to us?

MOHAN. Soon the rains will come. We will go back to our land and start again. The rains will come and it will be like before.

PARVATI. Start again? How many more times must we start again?

She turns away to return to the jhuggis. MOHAN *looks around to make sure he is safe and then departs. The cement mixer now takes on an eerie life of its own, turning and grinding in the dark. A* WOMAN *comes to stand beside it, her hand touching its drum, her head bent towards it. It's* KAMLA. *She's holding her baby. Slowly the drum stops turning.*

KAMLA (*to audience*). People may ask, why are you going to so much trouble for an unborn child. Why care where Asha's child is born? Why should we care if it is born at all? Is it not in your mind that we people have too many children as it is? More mouths to feed? We know about Sterilisation Programmes. These teams they come in shining jeeps to give us the operation. As they reach into us to take out our future children we sing the song they have taught us:

(Sings) A pruned tree is upright and beautiful.
Plump is the fruit and sweet.
Strong are the branches and roots
Of the tree that is pruned – carefully.
Judiciously.
The fruit is plump and the branches are strong.
Strong and beautiful . . .

A pause.

We know another song, another story. There's a fruit in the
desert. It comes from a small stunted tree. It grows only
where other trees cannot grow. The fruit is small. Often it is
dry inside and you have to throw it away. But when you find
a good one, you can hardly bear to eat it. It tastes of paradise.
Some people from outside came and took pieces of this tree
and they did things to it. They gave it better food and soil.
They chose only the best cuttings to plant again. You can now
buy this fruit in the shops. It is big and looks beautiful. It is
expensive. It tastes of nothing.

The cement mixer turns again. Dark. Sound of applause.
Spotlight leads in MOHINI, *glamorously attired and with a*
microphone and notes.

MOHINI. Thank you ladies and gentlemen. Thank you. I hope
we've all had a good time. I know I couldn't dance another
step. A special thanks to everyone who has supported this
event. *(Applauding.)* Thank you your Highness for lending
us the prestige of your presence this evening, for endorsing
our project with your kind words and enthusiasm not only
here but just as importantly abroad. A big thank you also to
you people who are in power at the moment – the politicians
– Left, Right and Centre – we don't take sides, we need
support from you all on this fund raising occasion. Applause
too for the Administrators, the Press and TV people on whom
we rely to spread the word about our aims and dreams, thank
you all and a special thanks to the business community,
the banks, developers, contractors, all you kind people
who have helped us to raise funds, to bring a little more
hope, a little more vision, a little more imagination to a fact
we all have to face. In this country there are three hundred
and fifty million people living below the poverty line in six
hundred thousand villages. Rural Development has to be

professionalised. We can no longer sit back helplessly declaiming 'India is a very poor country'. The poor will not be patient with us for ever. Chaos and catastrophe lurk in the streets. We're not miracle workers. We simply aim to help and keep them at bay. It's clearly in everyone's interests that we succeeed. We've made a beginning. We hope we can continue to rely on your encouragement and support. In the meantime we intend to screw you for every roop in your pocket!

The spotlight follows her off stage.

Bright lights. Orange and blue muslin screens suggest rural Rajasthan. We are now some miles from ASHA's village where her mother CHARU waits for her at the side of the road. Some yards away is a very OLD MAN in a huge turban who seems to be in a trance.

CHARU. Two days I've been waiting here. Asha has not come. There can be many reasons. Travelling is not easy. Sometimes there are bad crashes. Sometimes there are bandits. Sometimes the buses break down and a spare part has to be found before it can be mended. Once a bus was set alight. Sometimes there is flooding or sand drifts. Depending on the season.

OLD MAN. Sometimes the bus doesn't arrive because it has never departed.

CHARU. Two days we've been waiting for my daughter Asha. (*She displays it.*) This odhni I have made for her. A daughter should have her first child in the shade and coolness of her mother's house. A mother is entitled to the return of her own daughter to witness the birth. Tenderness is needed. Who can give this, if not her own mother? Some lorries have passed on the top road. There has been no news of a bus. Two days I've been waiting here. Asha has not come.

She sets out the odhni, a piece of fruit and some roti on a leaf.

Yesterday a strange woman carrying a bag with many buckles came from the road where the bus turns. This strange woman she sat down to ask questions. She had the look of the possessed. Like a woman who cannot sleep for the fear of dreams. Her lips were dry but she was not thirsty. Dust covered her head but she would not brush it off. She was not in her own world. What was it she asked?

OLD MAN. She was searching for the poorest people.

CHARU. Many such people have come this way. They have plans and dreams to change our lives. They have such wonderful ideas. We listen and we smile. But our dreams are not to do with them. Our dreams are only of rain.

OLD MAN. She wanted to live amongst the poorest.

CHARU. We sent her North. We are not the poorest. Some months ago our bullock died. Waiting for rain we have been pulling the plough with our own shoulders. But we are not the poorest. We have weeded out the thorns with our bare hands. We have moved the large stones to the edge of the field. In a tin drum, on a stone shelf, so that the rats will leave it be, we keep seed. There is now only enough for one sowing. Our first we lost. We were cheated by false rain. It came in the night heavy and loud. In the morning the pale soil was a beautiful rich mud. Carefully we sowed our seed. Inserting it, just so, not too deep, but covered enough to protect it from the sun. We waited for more rain to open the walls of the seeds, to push the shoots up into the light, to thicken and swell the stems. It didn't come. We have seen no rain since.

OLD MAN. The bridegroom ran away on his wedding night.

CHARU. That crop is now lost. If the rains continue to fail we will have to make food from the remainder of our seed. There is nothing else to eat. But we are not the poorest.

She rearranges the food and odhni.

This is all I have to give my daughter. In my house there is nothing. A pitcher of water and a handful of salt. She will give birth to her child in the room I have prepared. The walls have been whitewashed, but there will be no mithai, no singing. The old are sucking stones and the young are crying. And seven days after the child is born I will tell her. 'You must put the child on your back and return. Go back to the city my daughter where at least there is some food, here there is only dryness and dust. What else can I do?

OLD MAN. Our skins are flaked and our heels are cracked. We dream only of rain. Let the rains come.

CIIARU. Let the rains come, so my daughter can rest in my house and her child know its grandmother's voice: let the rains come so the trees know their leaves again, the land its crops, and the well its depth.

Ends.